# ALL about Wild ANiMaLS

# GIRAFFES

Please visit our web site at: **www.garethstevens.com**
For a free color catalog describing Gareth Stevens Publishing's list of high-quality books and multimedia programs, call 1-800-542-2595 (USA) or 1-800-387-3178 (Canada). Gareth Stevens Publishing's fax: (877) 542-2596

Library of Congress Cataloging-in-Publication Data available upon request from publisher. Fax (877) 542-2596 for the attention of the Publishing Records Department.

ISBN-10: 0-8368-4116-6   ISBN-13: 978-0-8368-4116-9 (Lib. Bdg.)

This edition first published in 2004 by
**Gareth Stevens Publishing**
A Weekly Reader Company
1 Reader's Digest Rd.
Pleasantville, NY 10570-7000 USA

This U.S. edition copyright © 2004 by Gareth Stevens, Inc. Original edition copyright © 2002 by DeAgostini UK Limited. First published in 2002 as *My Animal Kingdom: All About Giraffes* by DeAgostini UK Ltd., Griffin House, 161 Hammersmith Road, London W6 8SD, England. Additional end matter copyright © 2004 by Gareth Stevens, Inc.

Editorial and design: Tucker Slingsby Ltd., London
Gareth Stevens series editor: Catherine Gardner
Gareth Stevens art direction: Tammy Gruenewald

Picture Credits
NHPA — William Paton: cover and title page; Nigel J. Dennis: 6, 8, 20, 21; Rich Kirchner: 6-7; Martin Harvey: 7, 17, 18, 23, 27; Kevin Schafer: 9; Daryl Balfour: 9, 11, 13, 15, 18, 21, 27; Anthony Bannister: 9, 17, 24-25, 29; T. Kitchin and V. Hurst: 10, 13; Julie Meech: 14; Gerard Lacz: 17, 26; E. A. Janes: 19; Stephen Krasemann: 19, 28; Mike Lane: 22; Dr. Eckart Pott: 25; G. I. Bernard: 29.
Oxford Scientific Films — Mark Hamblin: 9; Steve Turner: 10-11; Norbert Rosing: 12; Bob Bennett: 15; Martyn Colbeck: 16; Philip Sharpe: 21; George Calef: 23; John Downer: 23; Alan Root: 28.

All rights reserved. No part of this book may be reproduced, stored in a retrieval system, or transmitted in any form or by any means, electronic, mechanical, photocopying, recording, or otherwise, without the prior written permission of the copyright holder.

Printed in the United States of America

2 3 4 5 6 7 8 9 08 07

# All about Wild Animals

# GIRAFFES

**Gareth Stevens**
Publishing

# Giraffe Facts

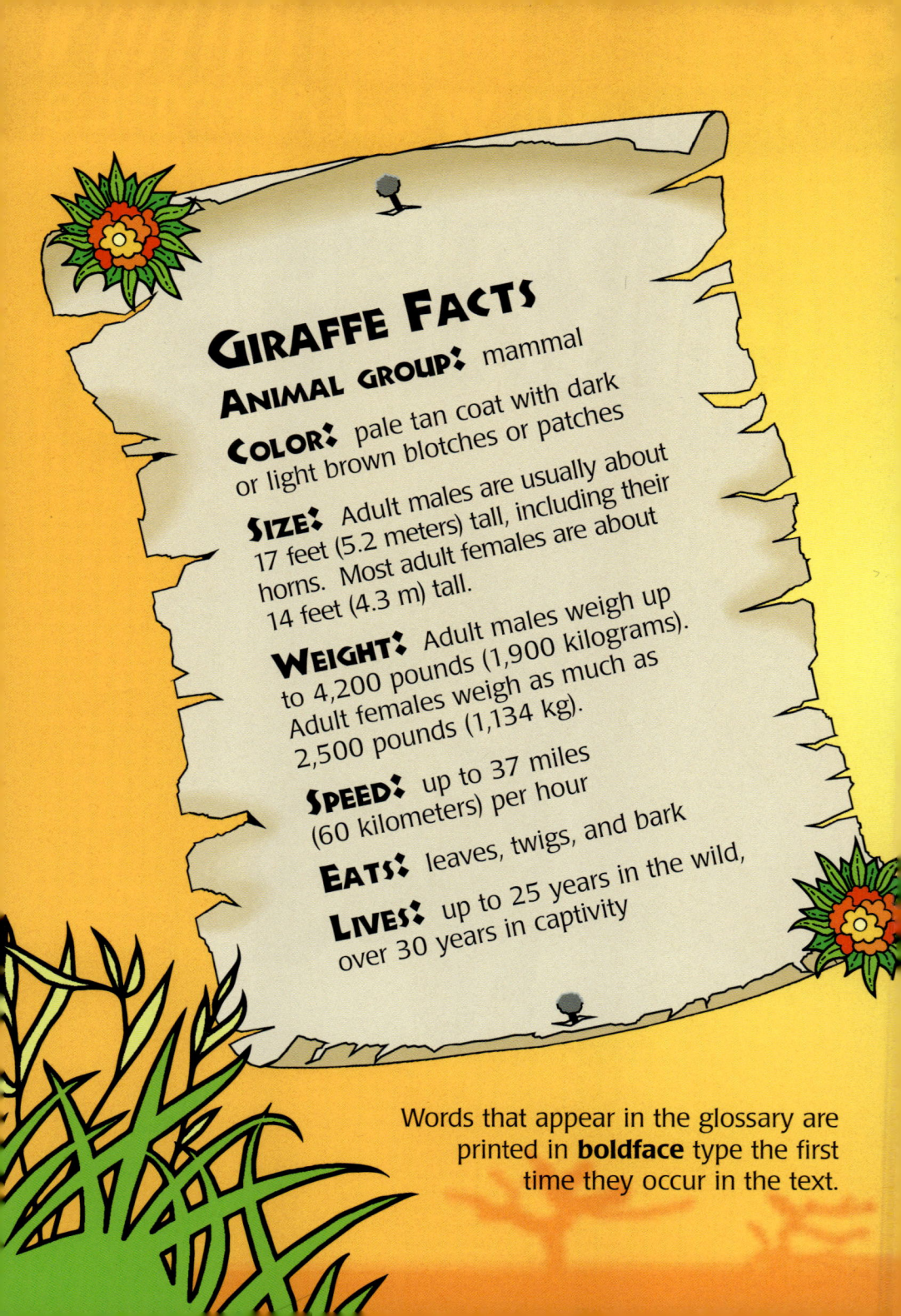

**Animal group:** mammal

**Color:** pale tan coat with dark or light brown blotches or patches

**Size:** Adult males are usually about 17 feet (5.2 meters) tall, including their horns. Most adult females are about 14 feet (4.3 m) tall.

**Weight:** Adult males weigh up to 4,200 pounds (1,900 kilograms). Adult females weigh as much as 2,500 pounds (1,134 kg).

**Speed:** up to 37 miles (60 kilometers) per hour

**Eats:** leaves, twigs, and bark

**Lives:** up to 25 years in the wild, over 30 years in captivity

Words that appear in the glossary are printed in **boldface** type the first time they occur in the text.

# CONTENTS

**A Closer Look** .........................6

**Home, Sweet Home** ...................10

**Neighbors** ............................12

**The Family** ...........................14

**Life on the Savanna** ..................18

**Favorite Foods** .......................20

**Danger!** ..............................22

**A Giraffe's Day** ......................24

**Relatives** ............................26

**Humans and Giraffes** .................28

**Glossary** .............................30

**Index** ................................32

# A Closer Look

Giraffes are the tallest animals on Earth. Their towering height lets them eat juicy leaves that are too high for other animals to reach. Adult male giraffes can grow to be more than 16 feet (5 meters) tall. Most humans are not even as tall as a giraffe's 6-foot (2-m) leg! A giraffe's height comes mainly from its super-long legs and neck. A full-grown male weighs as much as a small car, but the main part of its body is only about the size of a horse's body.

A baby giraffe is born with hair-covered horns. They lie flat against the giraffe's head, at birth, but stand upright in about a week.

My shoulders are higher than my hips, so my body slopes from front to back.

I have a tuft of stiff hair at the end of my long tail. It makes my tail great for swatting flies!

My long, powerful legs help me reach high for food and gallop away from danger.

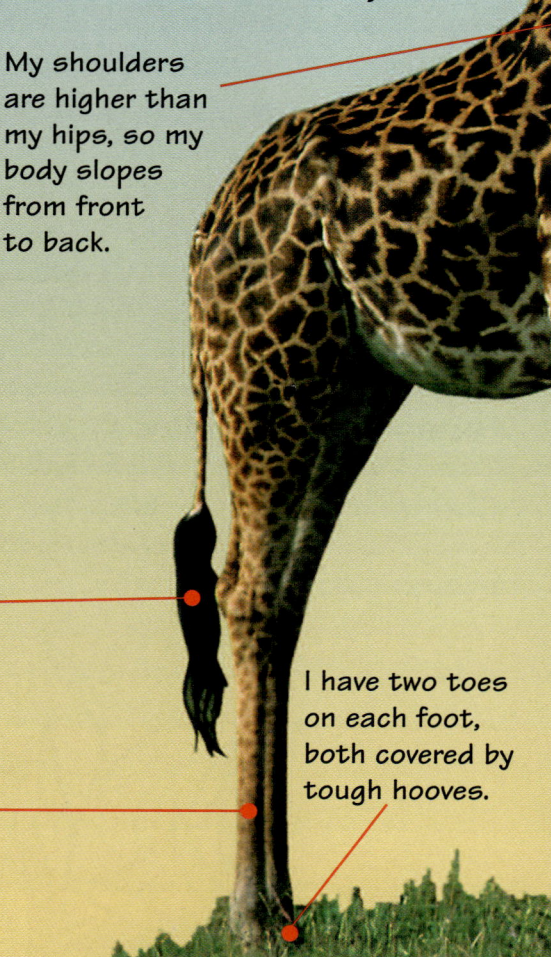

I have two toes on each foot, both covered by tough hooves.

I have large
eyes and
sharp vision.

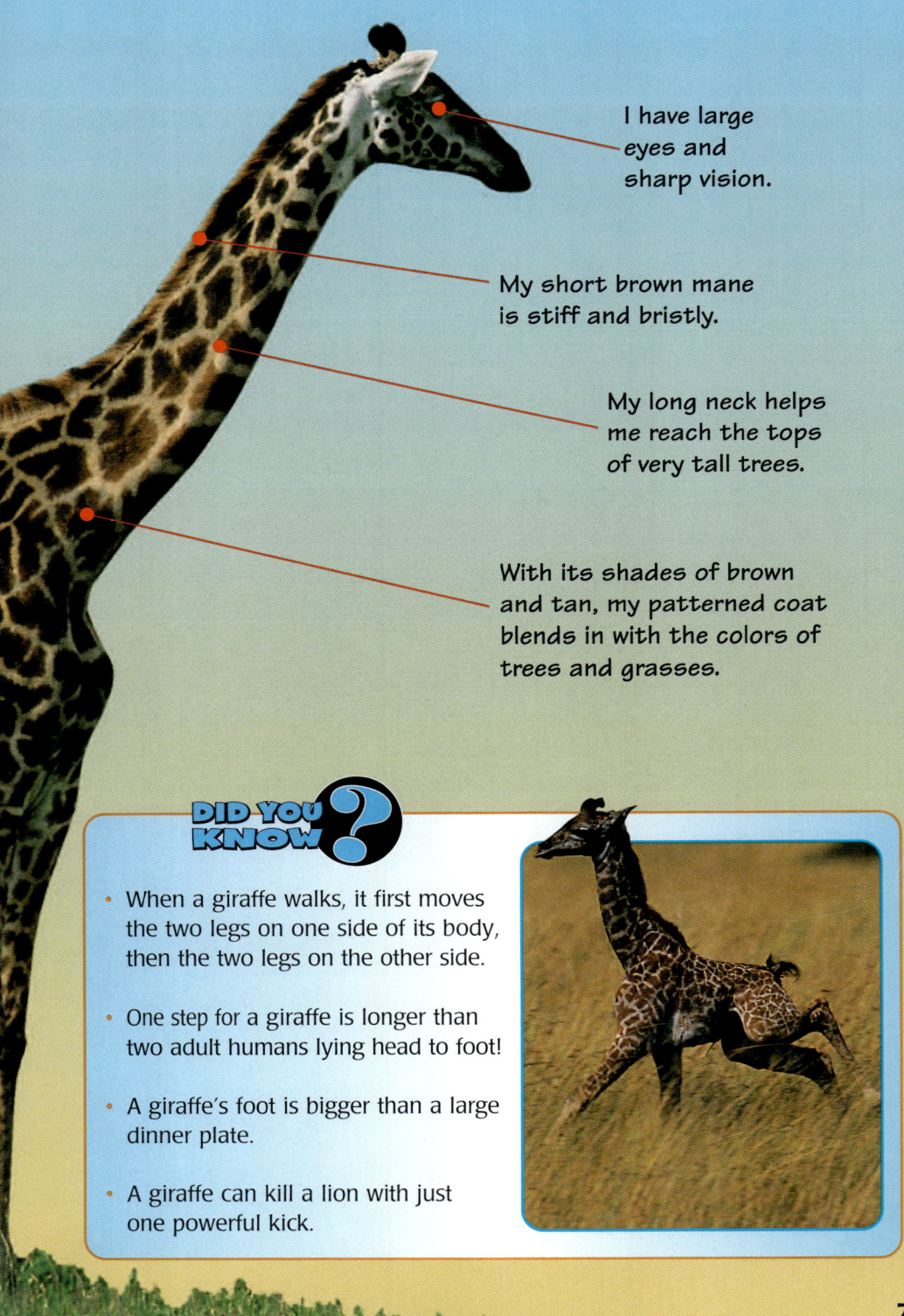

My short brown mane
is stiff and bristly.

My long neck helps
me reach the tops
of very tall trees.

With its shades of brown
and tan, my patterned coat
blends in with the colors of
trees and grasses.

## DID YOU KNOW?

- When a giraffe walks, it first moves the two legs on one side of its body, then the two legs on the other side.

- One step for a giraffe is longer than two adult humans lying head to foot!

- A giraffe's foot is bigger than a large dinner plate.

- A giraffe can kill a lion with just one powerful kick.

For their size, giraffes have small heads. Nevertheless, they hear, smell, and see very well, and they can sense danger from a long way off.

Both males and females have two or four short, blunt horns on their heads. The horns are covered with skin and, except at the ends, with hair. Some giraffes also have a hornlike bump between their eyes. Male giraffes use their horns to fight and to push each other. Females have shorter horns than males, and they do not fight.

## TWISTING

Giraffes have long narrow **muzzles** and flexible, **prehensile** tongues, which they use for reaching into bushy trees to pull off tasty leaves. A giraffe's tongue is pink and black, and it stretches up to 20 inches (50 centimeters), which is longer than a child's arm. To eat, a giraffe winds its tongue around a bunch of leaves, gripping them tightly. Then the giraffe pulls its head away, tearing the leaves off the tree.

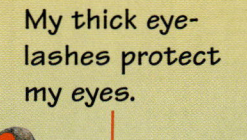

My bony horns are covered with skin and hair, but, over time, the hair at the tips usually wears away.

My thick eyelashes protect my eyes.

My eyes are on the sides of my head, so I can see all around me.

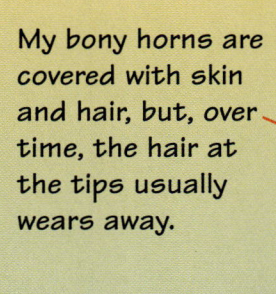

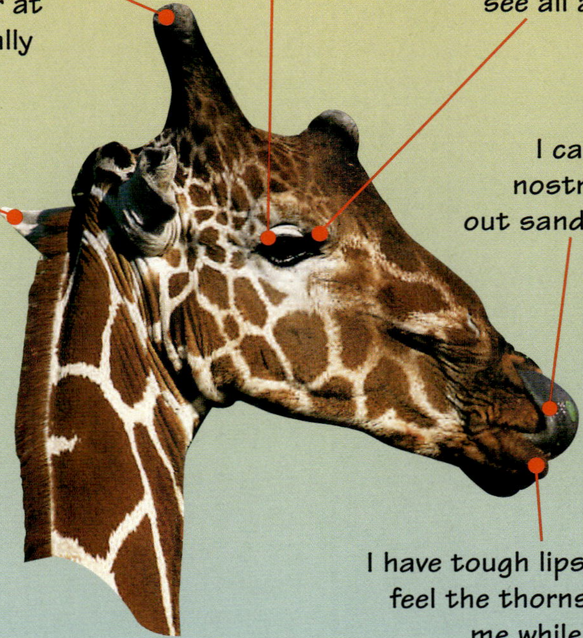

I can turn my large, pointed ears to hear the smallest sounds.

I can close my nostrils to keep out sand and dust.

I have tough lips, so I don't feel the thorns that poke me while I'm eating.

## Getting to Know You

Each giraffe has its own special markings on its coat. No two coats look exactly the same. The members of a herd use the markings, along with each giraffe's **unique** body scent, to tell each other apart. Immediately after her baby is born, a mother giraffe learns to recognize its smell and the pattern on its coat.

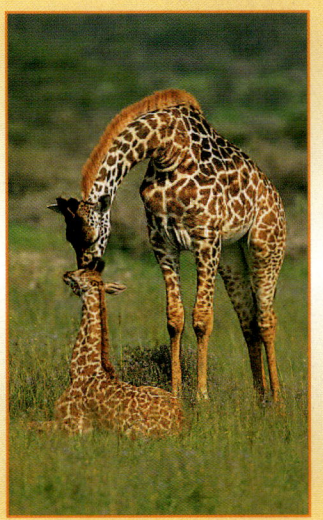

# Home, Sweet Home

Giraffes live in the open woods and on the **savanna**, or wooded grasslands, of southern Africa. The savanna has only two seasons, a wet season and a dry season. During the dry season, it sometimes does not rain for months, and giraffes may go for weeks without a drink of water. They get water from their food, however, and the **acacia** trees they like best do not need a lot of water to survive.

## Hiding Away

Although giraffes are very tall, they can still be hard to see in the wild, especially when they are standing near trees. The colors and patterns of their coats blend in perfectly with the shadows of leaves and branches.

## DID YOU KNOW?

- A giraffe's neck is much longer than a human's, yet both have only seven bones, or **vertebrae**. Each of a giraffe's neck bones is about sixteen times longer than a human neck bone.

- The word *giraffe* comes from the Arabic word *zirafah*, which means "the tallest of all."

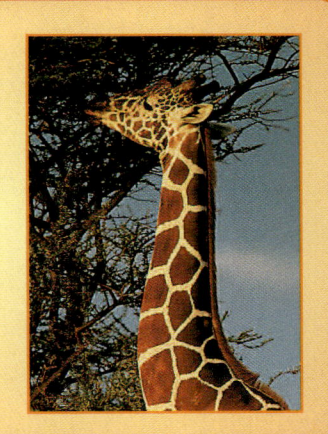

## Where in the World?

Giraffes live only in Africa, south of the Sahara Desert. They are most common in the eastern and southern parts of Africa. As people take over more and more wild areas for cities and farms, giraffes are being squeezed onto less and less land. Twenty-five million years ago, the ancestors of today's giraffes roamed across all of Africa, Europe, and Asia. Over these millions of years, the animal's physical features have changed a lot. In fact, some giraffes that lived in Africa ten million years ago were even taller than the giants that live there now.

# Neighbors

Giraffes share the savanna with lots of other big animals. More kinds of large wild animals live on the African savanna than in any other place in the world. Herds of antelope, elephants, zebras, and gnus roam the plains and **graze** on the grasses and leaves that grow there. The savanna is also home to fierce **predators** that need meat to survive. Groups of lions and hyenas will stalk even large **prey**, including giraffes.

## Special Spots

Up in the branches of a tree, a leopard can snooze the day away, but, while the leopard might look like a big, sleeping cat, it could actually be a hungry hunter, hiding in the tree's leafy shadows. Predators that like to hunt alone, such as leopards and cheetahs, usually stalk young giraffes that wander too far away from their mothers. Lions, on the other hand, hunt in large groups. Together, they can go after adult giraffes.

## Eat Up!

The elephant is the only other savanna animal that feeds on leaves at the tops of tall trees. It uses its long trunk to gather the leaves. When an elephant cannot reach the leaves, it may pull off a whole branch or even push over the entire tree.

## Feathered Friends

Small birds called oxpeckers will often hitch a ride on a giraffe's back. These birds gobble up the tiny, biting insects that live in the giraffe's coat. Both animals benefit. The giraffe gets rid of unwanted pests, and the bird gets a tasty meal! Oxpeckers will also sound a shrill call if they notice a predator nearby.

# The Family

Giraffes live in groups, or herds, of up to twenty animals. On the move or resting, each animal in the herd faces a different direction to keep a sharp lookout for danger. Although giraffes usually do not travel far during their lives, they are always moving from place to place to find fresh food. Herds do not have leaders, and the members of a herd do not stay together very long. As a herd moves around, many of the giraffes wander off and join other groups. Sometimes, herds split up into smaller groups. Females often form herds to help each other look after their young, and young males also form herds of their own.

15

A female giraffe, called a cow, returns to the same area every time she gives birth. A cow usually has only one baby, or calf, at a time. Giraffes rarely have twins. Calves are usually born at the start of the rainy season, when food is easier to find, and the mothers are able make rich milk for their babies. Young giraffes grow quickly and can leave home when they are three or four years old.

## Knotted Necks

When male giraffes, called bulls, look for female mates, fights often break out. Fighting bulls stand side by side and swing their long necks toward each other. They hit and bump each other with their horns, heads, and necks to see which giraffe is the strongest. Sometimes, their necks get tangled up, or one of the giraffes is knocked **unconscious**, but, usually, neither animal really gets hurt. The loser just walks away. Female giraffes do not fight each other, but they will kick any other animal that attacks them.

## Six Months to One Year

A young calf moves around and feeds with its mother's herd. It will eat green plants more and more, but until it is nine or ten months old, it will keep drinking its mother's milk, too. During its first year of life, a giraffe calf will grow about 3 feet (1 m).

## Two to Four Years

Female giraffes are fully grown and can have babies at four or five years old. A grown female will join a nearby herd and stay in the area where she was born. Young males leave at about three years old and form herds with other bulls, but a male may not be fully grown until age seven.

# Baby File

## Birth

Right after giving birth, a cow cleans her calf and gets to know how it looks and smells. By the time it is an hour old, the calf can stand on its wobbly legs and drink its mother's milk. A giraffe cow hides her calf in the bushes to keep it safe while she feeds. After about a week, the calf can nibble grass, and by four months, it can eat leaves.

## Big Baby!

On the day it is born, a baby giraffe is bigger than many full-grown humans. A calf is about 6 feet (2 m) tall and can weigh up to 150 pounds (68 kilograms), but next to its mother, it looks small.

# Life on the Savanna

Giraffes spend most of their time eating or searching for food. They are peaceful, quiet animals that do not often use their voices. Occasionally, they will make soft moans, snorts, or grunts, and calves will **bleat** when they want attention. Instead of noises, giraffes use the way they hold their necks and tails to send messages. If a predator is near, a giraffe will walk stiffly, with its head held high and its neck stretched out. Giraffes are **timid** animals but stay alert to danger.

## Doing the Splits

A giraffe can live for weeks without drinking water. It gets a lot of water from the leaves it eats. When water is easy to find, a giraffe drinks every two or three days. It can drink up to 50 quarts (47 liters) of water at a time. To drink, the giraffe has to spread its legs wide apart before it can lower its head. This awkward position makes it easy for a predator to attack.

## Leap Away

When a giraffe is in danger, it gallops away at speeds of up to about 37 miles (60 kilometers) per hour. Its gallop is a series of long leaps, and, as it gallops, its neck sways backward and forward.

## Brief Sleep

A giraffe sleeps deeply for only about five minutes at a time. It usually sleeps in a standing position, bending its neck backward in an arch to rest its head behind its back legs. Lying down, a giraffe is helpless — and it takes about ten minutes for it to stand up again! So when a giraffe is either napping or drinking, other giraffes watch the savanna for signs of danger.

# Favorite Foods

Giraffes eat a lot. In one day, they can gobble up more than 75 pounds (34 kg) of food, which is about the same weight as two hundred large apples. Giraffes munch on the leaves, bark, flowers, and fruits of about one hundred different kinds of plants, but their favorite food comes from acacia trees. Acacia leaves are three-quarters water, and they contain almost all of the **nutrients** a giraffe needs to stay fit and healthy.

## Let's Share

Giraffes feed on leaves that most other animals cannot reach or do not care to eat. Because taller males eat the leaves near the tops of trees, while shorter females can usually reach only the lower branches, both males and females can feed on the same tree and still get enough to eat. To get the leaves off of trees, a giraffe wraps its long, prehensile tongue around a bunch of leaves and rips them off the branch. Then, it covers its mouthful of food with sticky spit to make the leaves easier to swallow.

## Acacia Picnic

An acacia tree has long, sharp thorns that poke any animal trying to nibble on its leaves. A giraffe's long tongue can reach through the thorns. A giraffe also has very tough lips with a thick fringe of hair for protection. Even when a giraffe gets past the thorns, however, stinging ants on the acacia tree can still ruin its meal. The giraffe will put up with their biting for a while, then move on.

### DID YOU KNOW?

- A giraffe has four stomachs to help it break down the tough food it eats.

- Like people, giraffes need calcium to keep their bones and teeth strong. Some scientists think giraffes get calcium by chewing up the bones of dead animals.

## Salt, Please

Plants give giraffes most of the nutrients they need, but plants do not provide enough salt. To get more salt, giraffes find natural salt deposits, then lick up all the salt they need.

# Danger!

Full-grown giraffes are too big to have many enemies, except humans, but young giraffes are easy meals for lions, leopards, hyenas, and wild dogs. At the first sign of danger, a calf runs under its mother's body, but it is careful to keep out of the way of her hooves. A mother protects her calf by kicking with her strong legs. If a mother giraffe is too far away from her calf, however, she might not be able to save it. Half to three-quarters of all giraffe calves die in their first few months of life.

## Silent Hunter

A Nile crocodile lies, unseen, in the muddy water along a riverbank. A giraffe calf that is bending down to drink is no match for the crafty crocodile. The powerful reptile grabs the calf in its strong jaws and pulls it under the water until the calf drowns.

## Fatal Females

Lions are a giraffe's main predators. Especially when it is bending down to drink, an adult giraffe is easy prey for a **pride** of lions. Female lions, called lionesses, usually work together to attack a giraffe. One creeps close and pounces, knocking the giraffe to the ground. Then the rest of the pride moves in to make the kill and enjoy the feast.

### Pack Attack!

African painted dogs hunt in packs, and a lone giraffe calf is easy for these fierce hunters to attack. The barking, growling dogs hurl themselves at the calf, then pull it to the ground.

# A Giraffe's Day

**5:00 AM** — It was almost dawn. I was standing guard over my sleeping calf. I had hidden her in the bushes, but you can't be too careful with young calves when lions are prowling around.

**8:00 AM** — My calf and I ate some juicy shoots for breakfast. Then we wandered to the riverbank for a drink of water. One of the other adults in the herd kept a lookout for lions while we drank.

**10:00 AM** — We left with a few of our friends from the herd to find some more food. Along the way, we stopped to watch a group of young males pretending to fight like the adult males.

**12:00 NOON** — It was hot. I **nursed** my calf as we rested in the shade of the acacia trees. When she became restless, we joined a group of females and their babies.

**2:00 PM** — Two females watched the calves while the rest of us mothers went off on our own to find more food.

**5:00 PM** — Spotting a lioness, I snorted a warning. I stared at her, stretching my neck high. When she crept closer, we galloped away.

**6:00 PM** — The sun was setting. It would soon be dark. We stopped at some acacia trees for an evening meal.

**10:00 PM** — All was quiet. I laid down to take a short nap. Other adults stayed alert to watch for danger.

**12:00 MIDNIGHT** — The savanna was quiet, but my calf was restless. She needed to nurse again.

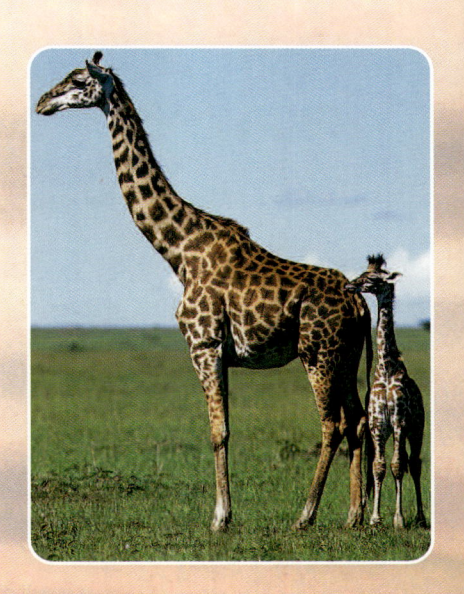

**2:00 AM** — Hidden in the bushes, the calves slept soundly. Some of the adults slept, too. I grazed, listening carefully for any sounds of danger.

**4:00 AM** — It will soon be dawn. I think I will take a quick snooze before my calf and I start our daily search for food.

# Relatives

About nine different kinds of giraffes exist in the world, today, living mostly in different parts of Africa. You can tell them apart by their coat patterns. The giraffe's only other close family relative is the okapi. Long ago, both giraffes and okapis roamed throughout most of Africa. Today, okapis are found only in the dense forests of central Africa. Both giraffes and okapis have big eyes and ears and long, flexible tongues. They have long tails, necks, and legs, for their size, but an okapi is much smaller than a giraffe. An adult okapi is only as tall as a newborn giraffe.

## OK Okapi

This unusual-looking creature has the horns of a giraffe, the head of a deer, the neck of a horse, and legs like a zebra's. The okapi also has a very long tongue, which it uses to feed and clean itself. It can even lick its eyes with its tongue! This relative of the giraffe lives in the forests of the Zaire region in central Africa.

## Distant Relatives

Giraffes and okapis belong to a big group of animals that also includes deer, antelope, and cattle. The members of this group are **ruminants**, or animals that chew **cud**. The leaves and other plant foods they eat start to break down in the stomach, then come back up into the mouth. The partly digested food, called cud, is softened with spit, then chewed and swallowed again.

### DID YOU KNOW?

- Ancient Romans thought that the giraffe's mother was a camel and its father was a leopard, so they called the giraffe a camel-leopard. This name led to the scientific name *Camelopardalis*.

- Giraffes and camels walk in the same way, and both can go a long time without water.

# Humans and Giraffes

The giraffe is known around the world for its height and its beautiful coat. It has been a favorite animal in zoos for thousands of years, and the constellation Camelopardalis gets its name from the giraffe. In the past, people hunted and killed giraffes for sport and forced them into smaller and smaller areas of land. Today, most giraffes live in protected parks or **game reserves** in Africa.

## Long Necks

Some groups of people in Africa have a custom of wearing many necklaces, all at the same time. The necklaces make their necks look very long and show that they are important people in their groups.

# Ancient Pictures

Archaeologists in Africa discovered these pictures of giraffes carved in rock. One of the giraffes is almost 20 feet (6 m) tall. The rock carvings, believed to be more than nine thousand years old, are extraordinary works of prehistoric art.

**DID YOU KNOW?**

Queen Hatshepsut of Egypt built the first zoo about 3,500 years ago. Collecting animals from all over Africa, she had a giraffe moved more than 1,500 miles (2,400 km) down the Nile River to her zoo. Today, giraffes are found in zoos all over the world.

# Glossary

## Acacia
A small tree or shrub that has feathery leaves and clusters of white or yellow flowers.

## Bleat
To make a weak, whiny sound like the cry of a sheep or a goat.

## Cud
Partly digested food that an animal has chewed, swallowed, and brought up from its stomach to chew again.

## Game Reserves
Areas of protected land where wild animals and plants can live in their natural habitats without being disturbed or harmed.

## Graze
To feed on growing plants.

## Muzzles
The noses and jaws that stick out at the front of animals' heads.

## Nursed
Fed on milk from the mother's body.

## Nutrients
The parts of foods that keep animals strong and healthy.

## Predators
Animals that kill other animals for food.

## Prehensile
Able to grasp something by wrapping around it.

## PREY
Animals that a predator hunts and kills for food.

## PRIDE
A group of lions.

## RUMINANTS
Animals that chew cud.

## SAVANNA
A large, flat grassland found in warm or tropical parts of the world.

## TIMID
Shy and easily frightened.

## UNCONSCIOUS
Not alert or able to see, feel, or think.

## UNIQUE
One of a kind; unlike any other.

## VERTEBRAE
The smaller bones that form a backbone.

# INDEX

acacia trees  10, 20, 21, 24, 25
Africa  10, 11, 26, 28, 29

calves  16, 17, 18, 22, 23, 24, 25
*camelopardalis*  27, 28
coats  7, 9, 10, 13, 26, 28
crocodiles  22

drinking  18, 19, 22, 23, 24

eating  6, 8, 9, 17, 18, 20, 21, 27
elephants  12, 13
enemies  22
eyes  7, 8, 9, 26

fighting  8, 16, 24
food  6, 10, 14, 16, 18, 20, 21, 24, 25, 27

galloping  6, 19, 24

hair  6, 8, 9, 21
hearing  8, 9
height  6, 28
herds  9, 14, 17, 24
horns  6, 8, 9, 16, 26

kicking  7, 16, 22

legs  6, 7, 17, 18, 19, 22, 26
leopards  12, 22, 27
lions  7, 12, 22, 23, 24
lips  9, 21

necks  6, 7, 11, 16, 18, 19, 24, 26, 28

okapis  26, 27
oxpeckers  13

predators  12, 13, 18, 23

salt  21
savannas  10, 12, 13, 18, 19, 25
sleeping  19, 24, 25
smelling  8, 9, 16
stomachs  21, 27

tails  6, 18, 26
tongues  8, 20, 21, 26

voices  18

walking  7, 27
water  10, 18, 20, 24, 27